Malcolm Dunn – Reflective

INDEX

In about 1971, I'd be about 15 years old, I heard Ralph McTell play his own composition "First Song" on the Michael Parkinson show and this performance proved to be a revelatory experience. I had always had a good singing voice and had been invited to join the Edinburgh Schools' Choir, an offer which, in my callow youth, I had not taken up. I also liked prose and poetry.

McTell's music continued to be influential and I began to play an old guitar which I used when singing my own songs.

On a few occasions my lyrics have been complemented by their comparison to poetry. However, when I was approached about a book of my lyrics, I was extremely flattered.

There were certain things discussed before putting pen to paper. One was whether the chorus should be left in or the lyrics "sanitised" for poetic purposes. I wasn't in favour of this because I felt that what should be published was what I had written. It was also pointed out that choruses are used in poetry and so this hurdle was easily overcome.

The other consideration was, should I include some notes as to the background of the words.

I liked the idea of having a conversation with the reader about the inspiration behind the words but didn't want to be too prescriptive about what interpretation should be made. Rather, like radio, people should form their own pictures and interpretations.

About the time I was approached about a book of my lyrics, I had been thinking about the change in music listening tastes and the fall away of album (cd) sales. I had decided to release a double album on cd of my own songs, to be called "Reflective".

It struck me that the book and album could in some way combine and so part one of the book (1 – 30) relates to the songs on the double album.

Part 2 (31 – 36) contains other lyrics that I like and Part 3 (37 – 41) consists of the lyrics from a concept album called "The Chronicles of Jacob Nuntis".

I suppose that lyric poetry with footnotes would be a fair description of this book, which I hope you will enjoy.

1. Bryan's Song

Struggling with my crossword, stuck on 21 across.
He came over to my table and asked if the seat was free, of course.
Started making small talk, about the weather and the rest.
Turned out he needed talking, to get something of his chest.

Life's a knife that cuts both ways, has a jagged edge.
You can watch it through the window or stand out on the ledge.

Getting nowhere with my cryptic, just waiting for my date
And as of course, just usual, she was already running late.
So, I had time for conversation, to hear his point of view
Though when I say conversation, really, I mean that listening
would do.

Life's a knife that cuts both ways, has a jagged edge.
You can watch it through the window or stand out on the ledge.

He said he'd tasted music and that he'd danced to the best
But time and tide betrayed him and now, it was time to rest.
But you can't go back down times old road and take another turn.
Memories are places you just never can return.

Life's a knife that cuts both ways, has a jagged edge.
You can watch it through the window or stand out on the ledge.

My lady finally showed and he said that he had to go.
He reminded me of someone in a sepia photo.
You don't betray what you believe if you get a second chance
To play the music in your heart, in your mind you still could still
dance.

Life's a knife that cuts both ways, has a jagged edge.
You can watch it through the window or stand out on the ledge.

My wife and I occasionally go to a café for lunch. On one occasion I was there trying to do the cryptic crossword in my newspaper, waiting for her to arrive. My peace was interrupted by a stranger who really just wanted to talk at me, possibly because he was lonely. He had lost his wife, who had also been his dance partner, and no longer danced because he didn't want to betray her memory, as if he thought that any enjoyment or fun he might have would be in some way be unfaithful. This started me thinking about older lonely people particularly those who have lost a life partner and are actually scared to be anything other than sad, in case they are disloyal to the memory of their loved one. So, Bryan's Song (it could have been any name) came about.

2. My Irish Girl

I travelled down to Campbeltown, took a ferry to Ballycastle.
Hitched down to The Ebb and Flow, stood out amongst the hustle.
I'd never been to Dublin town where stories are as large as life.
I'd travelled such a long, long way from my home back there in Fife.

I went down to Kilkenny, where the beer pours sweet and slow
And I breathed the air out on the street, watched the people come and go.
It had been a while since I last saw her and I wondered if she had changed.
I went to her home at 6 o'clock just as we'd arranged.

I'll travel by boat, I'll travel by car,
I'll follow your lead, I'll follow your star.
I'll tread on your heels, my head's a whirl.
All for the love of my Irish girl.

It was at a hurling shinty match that I first saw her face
And I noticed how she moved around with such elegance and grace.
And spending time in her company, I saw that she could thole
Even the dark Dunmore Cave, a place with so little soul.

I'll travel by boat, I'll travel by car,
I'll follow your lead, I'll follow your star.
I'll tread on your heels, my head's a whirl.
All for the love of my Irish girl.

She was just as I remembered with that smile and sparkling eyes
And she threw her arms around me, to my complete surprise.
It was a perfect summer and in the Nore, we found freshwater pearls.
I was at peace with myself, for the love of my Irish girl.

I'll travel by boat, I'll travel by car,

I'll travel by boat, I'll travel by car,
I'll follow your lead, I'll follow your star.
I'll tread on your heels, my heads a whirl.
All for the love of my Irish girl.

We married in September and the village drank dry the wine
We married in September and the village drank dry the wine
And we knew our living was going to be so rich and fine.
We travelled back to Scotland to my home town of Fife
So I could show my family my beautiful Irish wife.

I'll travel by boat, I'll travel by car,
I'll follow your lead, I'll follow your star.
I'll tread on your heels, my head's a whirl.
All for the love of my Irish girl.

A traditional style folk song telling the story of a Scottish lad who meets an Irish girl at a hurling/shinty international. They are immediately attracted and arrange to meet at her home in the summer. He goes back to Fife to sort out his affairs and then journeys to Kilkenny hoping he's doing the right thing. One day someone from Kilkenny will hear this song and may appreciate the local references!

3. Gentle is the Colour of Your Hand

Our love makes the time stand still between us.
Ever changing colour of the land.
Tends the garden of the season.
Gentle is the colour of your hand.

So sad for broken hearted promise.
Shattered crystal turns to sand.
Takes so long to find a reason.
Gentle is the colour of your hand.
Gentle is the colour of your hand.

It's always in those words eye-spoken.
It's in the tender of your touch.
Tousled hair upon my pillow.
These things that mean so much.

So sad for broken hearted promise.
Shattered crystal turns to sand.
Takes so long to find a reason.
Gentle is the colour of your hand.
Gentle is the colour of your hand.

Long hours ill advise the moment,
Missing simple pleasures of the land.
Our love makes the time stand still between us.
Gentle is the colour of your hand.

So sad for broken hearted promise.
Shattered crystal turns to sand.
Takes so long to find a reason.
Gentle is the colour of your hand.
Gentle is the colour of your hand.
Gentle is the colour of your hand.
Gentle is the colour of your hand.

I wrote this song when I was dating my wife. She lived a couple of hours travel away and because I had a dog, she did most of the travelling. Fortunately, she worked in London which was half way, so this helped a bit with her journeys. We had met in our 30s and I was thinking of distance and time in the context of our relationship. Also, my wife is a beautiful person who loves plants and birds and her garden. I thought of her gentle hands and nature and this song about her fell into place.

4. Lipstick Kisses

I had a house, built of glass.
Full of possessions, greener grass.
All that I wanted, gone are the days
'Til lipstick kisses showed me the way.

I had a girl I didn't have to pay
But there's no free lunches on a working day.
The price got too high, too high to stay.
Too much of a woman in every way.

Too hot to handle, dry as a bone.
You only get blood from a heart of stone.
It got so bad, I had to pray,
'Til lipstick kisses showed me the way.

I didn't know, she didn't say.
A house ain't a home when love is away.
I didn't know, she didn't stay.
I learned about lovin' while she was away.

Too hot to handle, dry as a bone.
You only get blood from a heart of stone.
It got so bad, I had to pray
'Til lipstick kisses showed me the way.

There was a time when every day
I'd wonder why my life was goin' this way.
It got it so bad, I had to pray
'Til lipstick kisses showed me the way.

Too hot to handle, dry as a bone.
You only get blood from a heart of stone.
It got so bad, I had to pray
'Til lipstick kisses showed me the way.

There was a time when I used to say

There was a time when I used to say
Tomorrow, tomorrow's, just another day.
Wasted time wishin' my life away
'Til lipstick kisses showed me the way.

Too hot to handle, dry as a bone.
You only get blood from a heart of stone.
It got so bad, I had to pray
'Til lipstick kisses showed me the way.

This is a song I wrote for a female singer friend of mine who had eventually found true love with another lady after a marriage that had not worked. She never recorded it but I liked the song so I adapted the words so that I could sing it. I suppose it's about true love versus material comfort.

5. Melanie's Song

Sometimes I miss you
The moment you have gone.
The touch and taste of you
Keeps lingering on.
Don't you know that I'm always thinking of you?
Don't you know that I'm always thinking of you?

Nothing else matters
When I'm lost in your arms.
Like a breeze that's gently swaying
Like a storm when it calms.
You give me times that no-one can take away.
You give me times that no-one can take away.

Why do you matter
More that all the others before?
I need you around me
Like the sea around a shore.
You are a time when no waves can shift the sand.
You are a time when no waves can shift the sand.

Feel like I'm falling,
Higher and higher.
Seems like I'm drowning,
Drier and drier.
Don't you know that I'm always thinking of you?
Don't you know that I'm always thinking of you?
Don't you know that I'm always thinking of you?

Usually people write love songs after meeting someone special. I wrote this song (I think I was still just in my teens) about the way I hoped I would feel about someone one day. Eventually I met Melanie in my 30s and the song finally made sense.

6. <u>Cinnamon Tears</u>

I didn't know you were serious,
Well how was I meant to tell?
You said it was for the fun of it
So I went along as well.
Now you cry those cinnamon tears.
Don't cry those cinnamon tears.
Sometimes memories run down my face,
Just like those cinnamon tears.

We can't talk when you've nothing to say
But I'm no villain of the piece.
Well, I was always straight with you.
Keep your memories they'll have to do.
And you cry those cinnamon tears.
Don't cry those cinnamon tears.
Sometimes memories run down my face,
Just like those cinnamon tears.

Don't want to leave on broken dreams
Or walk away on regrets.
We had such good times together
Must count for something yet.
Still you cry those cinnamon tears.
Don't cry those cinnamon tears.
Sometimes memories run down my face
Just like those cinnamon tears.

I hope I'll see you once again
And that time will mend.
You mean so much to me
I hope I'll see you again.
And you won't cry those cinnamon tears.
Don't cry those cinnamon tears.
Sometimes memories run down my face
Just like those cinnamon tears.
Just like those cinnamon tears.
Just like those cinnamon tears.

The word Cinnamon got into my head. I played around with the word for weeks before coming up with cinnamon tears. The phrase reminded me of the days when girls wore musk and henna was popular; when I was young. In those days there seemed to be an assumption (at least by parents) that relationships would end up in marriage (few did). As a result, a distinction started being made between 'loving someone' and 'being in love'. One couple I knew, the girl insisted that the relationship was "fine for now" but had no long-term future. The boy took her at her word and went off with someone else. There were tears and this became the basis for the song.

7. <u>Moonbeam in my Heart</u>

The little boy didn't stay for long.
She didn't know if she was strong enough
To keep going on.
Keep going on.

She said "I miss you so much my Angel boy.
I miss you so much my Angel boy.
It's just as painful to be apart
As the day I lost the moonbeam in my heart".

The little boy didn't stay for long.
They say that time heals but they are wrong.
It won't mend a hole in your heart.
The hole in a heart

She said "I miss you so much my Angel boy.
I miss you so much my Angel boy.
It's just as painful to be apart
As the day I lost the moonbeam in my heart".

The winds of time may run into years
And blow away the saddest tears.
They won't heal pain like this.
Heal pain like this.

She said "I miss you so much my Angel boy.
I miss you so much my Angel boy.
It's just as painful to be apart
As the day I lost the moonbeam in my heart".

The little boy didn't stay for long.
She wasn't sure she'd be strong enough
To carry on.
Keep going on.

She said "I miss you so much my Angel boy.

She said "I miss you so much my Angel boy.
I miss you so much my Angel boy.
It's just as painful to be apart
As the day I lost the moonbeam in my heart.
As the day I lost the moonbeam in my heart.
As the day I lost the moonbeam in my heart".

A friend posted a message about losing her baby son that inspired the song Moonbeam in my Heart. I cannot imagine the emotional trauma of losing a child. No parent should have to bury a son or daughter.

8. June's Song

It takes two to break a promise,
It takes two to start a fight
But it only takes one person
To sit alone at night.
Where were you when I needed you
When our last chance said goodbye?
And I was sitting with the embers
And I couldn't even cry.

Now you ask me to explain
But I've said it all before.
And time takes its toll of me
Still you're wanting more.
Can't you see that it's all over
It never did begin.
Don't think that you're the loser here
'Cause no-one seems to win.

Leaving seems so simple
You just turn and walk away.
And I feel I should say something
But there's nothing left to say.
It's no use you saying that you're lost
And want to come back home.
I know I never found you
I've always been alone.

I keep old photographs that friends
Say I shouldn't keep.
They bring reminders that stay
With me when I sleep.
And all that I remember now
Are my parting words to you.
Words that seem so simple,
Words will never do.

It takes two to break a promise,

It takes two to break a promise,
It takes two to start a fight
But it only takes one person
To sit alone at night.
Where were you when I needed you
When our last chance said goodbye?
And I was sitting with the embers
And I couldn't even cry.

Years ago, a friend was going through a bad time in a relationship. I said to a mutual friend that I was sad for what she was going through. They seemed unimpressed and replied that there were always two sides to a story, for instance it takes two to start a fight. However, I thought that it only takes one person to be alone and this song came to life.

9. <u>Jonquille</u>

Sickle, scythe, late summer heat bring all hands to the field.
Sheaves of corn dry in the sun, a hard but welcome yield.
If you kiss the sun good morning, if you kiss the sun goodnight,
If you sleep when it gets dark and waken in the light.

I'll let you wash over me.
I'll let you wash over me.
I'll let you wash over me, Jonquille.

Exhausting work is harvesting, sheaf makers tie the corn
Into sheaves and stand them out in stooks to dry in the warm.
Gleaners collect the leftovers, harvest fair was soon.
I was trying to catch her eye all that afternoon.

I'll let you wash over me.
I'll let you wash over me.
I'll let you wash over me, Jonquille.

Dreaming of a Sunday when the gathering is through
And we've made our mark and made our coin, now it's time for we
two.
The Service lesson tells us what we should do and say
But the cider wine and promise puts it off another day.

I'll let you wash over me.
I'll let you wash over me.
I'll let you wash over me, Jonquille.

The band was playing, the harvest supper was about to start.
The last of the corn brought from the field on a horse and cart.
Putting on my Sunday clothes, my working rags ain't right.
I'm going to make an impression on her tonight.

I'll let you wash over me.
I'll let you wash over me.
I'll let you wash over me, Jonquille.

The consequence of others,

The consequence of others, only speak when you are kind.
A flower that contains the sun that you can rarely find.
I was trying to catch her eye all that afternoon,
I'm going to make an impression on her soon.

I'll let you wash over me.
I'll let you wash over me.
I'll let you wash over me, Jonquille.
Jonquille.
I'll let you wash over me, Jonquille.

I had written a couple of songs of a similar genre and needed to change direction. I wanted to write a traditional style folk song. I did some research about the 19th Century harvests but was worried that I'd just end up copying Ralph McTell's 'The Girl From The Hiring Fair'. Anyway, "Scotland Revisited" came from nowhere and writing that song distracted me long enough to revisit the "harvest project" with a clear head. I had a neighbour when I lived in Gateshead who had a daughter named Jonquille. I always thought it a beautiful and unusual name and had decided to call my next album Jonquille. I felt that I needed a song of that name to go with the album title and this unlocked the trad folk style song I was looking for. It's a song about an itinerant worker during the "golden" harvest in the 19th century who has his eye on a young woman, Jonquille, who he hopes will attend the Harvest Supper (which was disapproved of by the Church as it became rather boisterous!) with him.

10. St Jude's Road

Down by the river where the big trees grow
You can only see the sun through the branches low.
Roots sticking out where the soil washed away,
When the river is angry you should just walk away.
Heard there was a prospector struck it rich.
My daddy made his money digging a ditch.

Didn't have shoes 'til I was nine or ten.
Some talk of school but that was then.
Stealing apples, catfish stew,
My Mama always knew just what to do.
Then my daddy died and I had to earn.
You got to stand up when it's your turn.

Down by the river where the big wheel drives,
Making power from water supplies.
Not much of a living, not much of a life,
A couple of kids and an angry wife.
Maybe I'll buy me an old gold pan,
Strike it rich be a lucky man.

Then came the men they were looking for oil.
They drilled deep holes in the farming soil.
There was work for some but it was more like toil.
The one who made some money just sold snake oil.
And maybe I'll count the blessings I can,
End up being like my old man.

They say things come to those who wait,
That's like fish just catching the bait.
Scraping a living, catching a dime,
Sliding down the ladder one rung at a time.
Pushing a plough, working by hand,
This is what they call the promised land.

Food on the table another day,

Food on the table another day,
Doing what you must to make it pay.
Drinking whiskey from a copper still.
Blue flame means it's safe to distil.
Gassed the car, stacked the load.
Another trip down St Jude's road.

Driving fast, driving hard.
You don't earn money in the prison yard.
Not much of a living not much of a life,
Got to earn money for the kids and wife.
Soup up the engine, stack the load.
Another trip down St Jude's road.

*St Jude is, amongst other things, the patron saint of lost causes.
Sometimes I feel that people are given no real chance due to their
circumstances. It's a bit "Huckleberry Finn" in concept I suppose.
Imagine there being little work and little money and the temptation
to drive illicit hooch down St Judes Road.*

11. Stubborn Curl

Now I don't regret many things that I have said or done.
I've even walked away from things when I knew that I had won.
But I do regret not meeting you when we'd arranged the time
And I wonder how things could have been if you were still mine.

And I wonder if you're married now, with perhaps a little girl
With your blue eyes and that stubborn blond curl.

It was 1992 or was it 1993?
My first glance was enough, you came 'round my house for tea.
And one thing led to another and we wrecked the bedroom.
I still remember the promise of your sweet perfume.

And I wonder if you're married now, with perhaps a little girl
With your blue eyes and that stubborn blond curl.

It's like a Saturday on a Sunday, like a parody of what's mine,
Like a make-believe of reality, like a cold forecast of fine.
Making marmalade from fruit, making wine from grapes.
Playing life just like a game for only table stakes.

And I wonder if you're married now, with perhaps a little girl
With your blue eyes and that stubborn blond curl.

You didn't walk in my shoes and I didn't walk in yours.
You let me have my beliefs, didn't judge my points of view.
I was reckless and you were straight, an ideal match you see
But my head was in the clouds and I was much too carefree.

And I wonder if you're married now, with perhaps a little girl
With your blue eyes and that stubborn blond curl.

Now I don't regret many things that I have said or done.
I've even walked away from things when I knew that I had won.
But I do regret not meeting you when we'd arranged the time
And I wonder how things could have been if you were still mine.

And I wonder if you're married now,

And I wonder if you're married now, with perhaps a little girl
With your blue eyes and that stubborn blond curl.
With your blue eyes and that stubborn blond curl.

There are a lot of songs and poems about regrets - "the road not taken" - "what if a different choice had been made" - "if you had your time again what would you do differently?" I was thinking about this and decided that if I had taken a different path I would not have ended up where I am and I am happy here. This led me to wonder what song of regret I would be writing if I had not married my wife and had let her get away. Fortunately, I didn't lose her but I thought I'd write the song anyway!

12. **<u>When The Bees Have Gone</u>**

So many people, mourning their loss.
So many busy roads still left to cross.
I'll bring you emeralds like your eyes so cold.
I'll bring you sweet words for your heart of gold.

Nobody's listening to points of view.
Original concepts that aren't that new.
When we were kids we'd swim in the river cold
And I'd whisper sweet words to your heart of gold.

When red skies linger like a fiery dawn,
Who'll bring you honey when the bees have gone?
Who'll bring you honey when the bees have gone?

Some days in castles, some days in clouds.
I seldom tell you, you make me proud.
If I set sail without you I would surely drown.
You are the music that won't ever let me down.

The moon is lingering in a fiery dawn.
Who'll bring you honey when the bees have gone?
Who'll bring you honey when the bees have gone?

There will be sky flames when the rain burns.
Wind twists, the weather turns.
There'll be no time when the clocks have stopped.
There'll be no bread when the stalks are cropped.

When red skies linger like a fiery dawn,
Who'll bring you honey when the bees have gone?
Who'll bring you honey when the bees have gone?

I'll bring you emeralds, like your eyes so cold.
I'll whisper sweet words to your heart of gold.
If I set sail without you I would surely drown.
You are the music that won't ever let me down.
You are the music that will never let me down.

My environmental song. When I was young, rivers were heavily polluted and we had coal fire- induced smog. This all was cleared up but we seem to be environmentally in a worse state. The words include reference to swimming in rivers when I was a kid, love and a heart of gold, other environmental problems and the person with cold green eyes watching the bees disappear.

13. Red Cent

Well, I read what you wrote me and I know I don't deserve
You giving me another second chance.
I'll get straight on that wagon on Monday morning'
I won't even give this place a second glance.

And I won't spend a red cent on Saturday night
Because I know how that will end.
I'll be up to my old tricks, down with my friends.
So, I won't spend a penny Saturday night.

It will be a long weekend 'til I can roll,
With temptation hot on my mind.
I know my friends will be down the bright lights
Where the women are soothing and kind.

So, I won't spend a red cent on Saturday night
Because I know how that will end.
I'll be up to my old tricks, down with my friends.
So, I won't spend a penny Saturday night.

It was kind what you wrote me and I know I don't deserve
You giving me another second chance.
I'll go straight on the wagon on Monday morning,
I won't give that girl a second glance.

And I won't spend a red cent on Saturday night
Because I know how that will end.
I'll be up to my old tricks, down with my friends.
So, I won't spend a penny Saturday night.

It's a shame there's no train until Monday at noon,
It's a long time for temptations fall.
But I'm going to be strong, I'll be resolute.
I'll ignore my friends when they call.

And I won't spend a red cent

And I won't spend a red cent on Saturday night
Because I know how that will end.
I'll be up to my old tricks, down with my friends.
So, I won't spend a penny Saturday night.
So, I won't spend a red cent Saturday night.
So, I won't spend a red cent Saturday night.

I was laid up after an operation and a friend dropped off his banjo to help me pass my recovery time. For some reason I was thinking about people who give (and are given) more than one last chance. It seems to me that if you blow previous chances, you're not that serious and the odds are that it doesn't really matter how many you're given, they are going to be blown! A song about second chances.

14. Oleander Butterfly

If I could take you dancing one more time.
If I could hear your dreams again, like you were still mine.
We could tear a hole in space, rip a hole in time.
We could make forever last, like you were still mine.

Oleander butterfly, such beauty, so sad.
Reminds me of our make believe,
Those times we never had.

If I could take you dancing on that big stage.
If we could sing that song again from off the same page.
We could make that music, the rhythm and the rhyme.
We could make sense of the words, like you were still mine.

Oleander butterfly, such beauty, so sad.
Reminds me of our make believe,
Those times we never had.

Baby, I've been wondering about the dragonfly.
If he can reinvent himself, then maybe so can I.
A sapphire dragonfly glinting in the sunshine.
We could make sense of the world, if you were still mine.

Oleander butterfly, such beauty, so sad.
Reminds me of our make believe,
Those times we never had.

If I could grow some wings then maybe I could fly.
If that old dragonfly can do it, then maybe so can I.
I could make things up to you, at least in time,
Then we could make forever last, like you were still mine.

Oleander butterfly, such beauty, so sad.
Reminds me of our make believe,
Those times we never had.
Those times we never had.

The atomic bomb was dropped on Hiroshima on 6 August 1945 and, although it was thought that nothing would grow there for 100 years, by the time spring of 1946 arrived, the landscape was dotted with the blooming red petals of the Oleander. A sign of hope for the future, whatever the circumstances. I thought of the Oleander like a butterfly emerging from the chrysalis and so came the name Oleander Butterfly. I was also reading about the metamorphosis of the dragonfly. Tennyson described a dragonfly splitting its old skin and emerging shining metallic blue like "sapphire mail" in his 1842 poem "The Two Voices". This led me to this song which is about hope, growth and second chances.

15. Scotland Revisited

I walked in the hills with my dad as a boy
Pretending I was just like Rob Roy.
I remember the ptarmigan that flew out of the gorse
And the capercaillie at the rivers source.

The purple of heather and the green of the glen.
I wonder when I'll go back again?

Walk the Lairig Ghru from Aviemore.
Camp out rough by the shore
Of the sweet clear water, on the river bank.
And the newspaper boat that immediately sank.

The purple of heather and the green of the glen.
I wonder when I'll go back again?

We cooked our tea on a paraffin lamp
And ate our beans like a cowboy camp.
Slept under canvas on lumpy ground,
Lulled to sleep by the rivers sound.

The purple of heather and the green of the glen.
I wonder when I'll go back again?

We walked up the Pony Track, my dad said we climbed.
The mountain with its head in the clouds all the time.
Put a stone on the cairn at the top of The Ben
So the mountain will remember me again.

The purple of heather and the green of the glen.
I wonder when I'll go back again?

The man of the mountain with the old rucksack
Comfortably hitched upon his back.
My dad said that he was the real McCoy,
I thought that was his name, well I was only a boy.

The purple of heather

The purple of heather and the green of the glen.
I wonder when I'll go back again?

The rescue hut and the clear blue sky.
The weather can change in the blink of an eye.
I remember that haven for those who walk
Through the valleys and hills of the Hawk.

The purple of heather and the green of the glen.
I know I'm going back again; I know I'm going back again.

*A song I wrote when I was 60 about a couple of holidays in
Scotland with my Dad when I was a boy. I don't know where the
thoughts came from as I was trying to write a completely different
song but the words fell into place almost writing themselves. It's a
pretty accurate description of events that actually happened on two
camping holidays.*

16. Don't Go Crying In Your Dreams

Walking on smoke, sliding on glass,
Soon the pain will begin to pass.
Words that float, don't mean a thing.
Those hidden thoughts in a frozen stream.

Don't go crying in your dreams.
Don't go crying in your dreams.

If you've had dark, then you know there's light.
There's no real peace when life's a fight.
Praying things are going to change,
Seeking order in a disarrange.

Don't go crying in your dreams.
Don't go crying in your dreams.

Once so close, a stranger now.
A left field changer, anyhow.
Reaching out in an empty room.
Hopelessness is a shadow's loom.

Don't go crying in your dreams.
Don't go crying in your dreams.

So what about what might have been!
Memories aren't quite what they seem.
Shadows on your sleeping mind.
Symbols never clearly redefined.

Don't go crying in your dreams.
Don't go crying in your dreams.

Strong caffeine and nicotine.

Strong caffeine and nicotine.
Sleeping pills and amphetamines.
Wishing for a time machine.
Wishing for what might have been.
Don't go crying in your dreams.
Don't go crying in your dreams.
Don't go crying in your dreams.
Don't go crying in your dreams.

This song is about using drugs as an emotional crutch

17. I'll Be Thinking Of You

Another breath on the water, a ripple in space.
Read a book I borrowed from you in the first place.
You could see in the painting, 'though your eyes have failed.
Another breath on the water, just before you sailed.

It's Church tomorrow and I'm thinking of you.
And a robin flew in and took some seed and I'm thinking of you.
When the daffodils bloom, I'm in a crowded room, I'm just
thinking of you.
I'm just thinking of you.

It's not goodbye, it's just some more loose change
And in your time, you've known that lots, so it's nothing strange.
Sketching out a new way, on a greeting card.
Another breath on the water, it's going to be real hard.

It's Church tomorrow and I'm thinking of you.
And a robin flew in and took some seed and I'm thinking of you.
When the daffodils bloom, I'm in a crowded room, I'm just
thinking of you.
I'm just thinking of you.

When you're ready to go and you ask me my permission to leave.
And it's time to move on, my heart has burst on my sleeve.
I want to say something; I'm not usually tongue-tied.
Another breath on the water, just want to hide.

It's Church tomorrow and I'm thinking of you.
And a robin flew in and took some seed and I'm thinking of you.
When the daffodils bloom, I'm in a crowded room, I'm just
thinking of you.
I'm just thinking of you.

Daffodils and Red Breasts,

Daffodils and Red Breasts, those riverside walks.
Sweet advice when I needed it, those long evening talks.
The metronome still ticking, doesn't leave a clue.
Another breath on the water, just thinking of you.

It's Church tomorrow and I'm thinking of you.
And a robin flew in and took some seed and I'm thinking of you.
When the daffodils bloom, I'm in a crowded room, I'm just
thinking of you.

I'm just thinking of you. I'm just thinking of you.
I'm just thinking of you. I'm just thinking of you.
I'm just thinking of you. I'm just thinking of you.
I'm just thinking of you.

*My mother-in-law was terminally ill and my wife asked me to write
a song about her. I ended up writing about their relationship and
the sense of loss.*

18. Angel of Spring

Angel of Spring, sun in her eyes.
The water ripples with her sighs.
Daffodil smiles, like sun in the rain.
I've waited so long to see her again.

Just trying to let Spring ease my blues away.
Just trying to let Spring ease my blues away.

The rain will cry but it won't weep.
Small steps of music, comfort to keep.
I've always moved on, heading for a fall.
If I wasn't with you, I'd be nowhere at all.

Just trying to let Spring ease my blues away.
Just trying to let Spring ease my blues away.

Sunshine smiles, laughter talks.
Midday sun and evening walks.
Like a sleeping child, so much at peace.
Pale sunsets of soft cerise.

Just trying to let Spring ease my blues away.
Just trying to let Spring ease my blues away.

Angel of Spring, sun in her eyes.
The water ripples with her sighs.
Daffodil smiles, like sun in the rain.
I've waited so long to see her again.

Just trying to let Spring ease my blues away.
Just trying to let Spring ease my blues away.
Just trying to let Spring ease my blues away.
Just trying to let Spring ease my blues away.

*People suffer from Seasonal Affective Disorder (**SAD**) which is sometimes known as "winter depression" because the symptoms are usually more apparent during the winter. This song is about the easing of **SAD** as the seasons change.*

19. Cut The Mustard

We travelled 'round Old England, a few and far between.
Harvesting the mustard, with scythes that were so keen.
Mustard was the main crop and a living could be had
If you could cut the mustard living wouldn't be that bad.
For a blunt scythe cuts no mustard
And a faint heart draws no card.
For if you can cut the mustard
Living needn't be that hard.

The Romans brought the mustard, Mrs Clements made it pay
And a flour mill in Norwich made it famous 'til this day.
It was cut by hand with scythes the same as hay.
The crop could grow to six feet high and take your edge away.
And a blunt scythe cuts no mustard
And a faint heart draws no card.
For if you can cut the mustard
Living needn't be that hard.

I'd have bet a shilling; I'd have even bet a pound
There was nowhere else better for the mustard to be ground.
You see I'd never found a place worth returning to.
I'd never ever found a place where staying on would do.
For a blunt scythe cuts no mustard
And a faint heart draws no card.
For if you can cut the mustard
Living needn't be that hard.

The cottage it had windows that were small but they were clean.
A shoebox of the sky with mustard sunshine in between.
And I could have moved along, left right there and then
But I'd have left the summer and I'd have left good friends.
For a blunt scythe cuts no mustard
And a faint heart draws no card.
For if you can cut the mustard
Living needn't be that hard.

So, I will stay here for a while,

So, I will stay here for a while, I'll maybe end my time.
For I can cut the mustard and I can take my thyme.
And I have friends and moving on's a habit I can break.
There's only so many new ways this old dog can take.

For a blunt scythe cuts no mustard
And a faint heart draws no card.
For if you can cut the mustard
Living needn't be that hard.
If you can cut the mustard
Living needn't be that hard.

I was wondering about the origins of this phrase and did some research. Although many of the explanations seem to have little or nothing to do with mustard, I came across references to the time when mustard was one of the main crops in East Anglia. It was cut by hand with scythes, in the same way as corn. The crop could grow up to six feet high and this was very arduous work, requiring extremely sharp tools. When blunt, they "would not cut the mustard". In the 18th century, with the developments in milling techniques, the husks could be more easily removed and the seeds finely ground. The first record of the production of mustard flour (the most common form of mustard used commercially) is credited to Mrs Clements of Durham in 1720 who managed to keep the milling technique used a secret for some time allowing Durham to become the centre of mustard production in the country and allowing herself to accumulate considerable sums of money selling her mustard flour.
Once her milling secret was discovered other entrepreneurs began to invest in mustard production. Most notable in the 19th century was Jeremiah Colman who began milling mustard at his flour mill in Norwich. With his brilliant marketing techniques his mustard became the quintessential English mustard – a finely milled flour, yellow in colour (assisted by the addition of turmeric) and very hot in taste.

20. My Valley Is My Sanctuary

Rowing a slow boat across the wide water.
Mountain mist on the loch.
The breath of the pines and the splash of an otter.
The whispering wings of the hawk.

In a world that crumbles from past failed solutions
A road with no turnings, you see.
I can hide me now from peaceful revolutions
My valley is my sanctuary.

If the Garden of Eden looked like these mauve mountains,
So lonely but never alone.
There's pleasure in peace as I row my slow boat
To the house that I still call my home

In a world that crumbles from past failed solutions
A road with no turnings, you see.
I can hide me now from peaceful revolutions
My valley is my sanctuary.

We've abolished slavery and ended the War.
Stopped child abuse and harm.
We brought about equality, stopped the exploitation
Of workers in factories and farms.

But a hundred years on things don't seem to have changed.
A sad reflection on progress, you see.
I can hide me now from civilised society
My valley is my sanctuary.

Rowing a slow boat across the wide water.
Mountain mist on the loch.
The breath of the pines and the splash of an otter.
The whispering wings of the hawk.

In a world that crumbles

In a world that crumbles from past failed solutions
A road with no turnings, you see.
I can hide me now from peaceful revolutions
My valley is my sanctuary.
My valley is my sanctuary.

I don't know about you, but sometimes when I hear the news and everything seems so desperate, I imagine going to a lonely cottage in the Highlands, away from it all where I can hide from the insanity. On one occasion, the news had reports celebrating the centenary of the emancipation of women, the War To End All Wars, abolition of slavery, fairness to factory workers, simultaneously with reports about the unfairness of comparative men/woman's salaries, the suppression of female workers, fixed hours contracts, illegal immigrants sold as sex slaves and wars in the Middle East. Surprisingly, it seemed that the media found this contradictory reporting perfectly reasonable.

21. Party

Evening said she'd write or 'phone
Then left me sitting on my own.
Has anybody got a light?
I couldn't help thinking of you tonight.

I know that it wasn't real
And I knew that you'd cry for the way I feel.
The party's gone and so's the wine
Can I have an hour of your time?

I know I've had too much to drink.
The lovers have gone as the evening sinks.
And now I've got those morning blues,
And I couldn't help these thoughts of you.

Evening said she'd write or 'phone
Then left me sitting on my own.
Has anybody got a light?
I couldn't help thinking of you tonight.

Feeling tired with talk that's cheap
If I closed my eyes, I'm sure I'd sleep.
Alone with people, friends of friends,
Sitting on a sofa like bookends.

I know I've had too much to drink.
The lovers have gone as the evening sinks.
And now I've got those morning blues,
And I couldn't help these thoughts of you.

Evening said she'd write or 'phone
Then left me sitting on my own.
Has anybody got a light?
I couldn't help thinking of you tonight
Of you tonight, of you tonight.

We used to go to parties when we were young often without knowing the person hosting the party. The picture I have in my mind is of a darkened room with earnest kissing couples and a brightly lit kitchen where most people were standing around drinking. There always seemed to be someone who nobody knew who had stayed after his girlfriend had left. Presumably their curfew times were different. I wondered what his story was and I wrote this song about him

22. Fish Ain't Biting

A rich man's gift is a poor man's treasure.
A poor man's gift is time to pleasure.
Each has a value equal in measure
But the fish ain't biting tonight.

The hens won't lay and the corn won't grow.
What's wrong with the seasons? Nobody knows.
Somethings up and it won't come down.
What goes around comes around.

May as well cut along right now,
I can't dance, it's too wet to plough.
Still I try, sweat on my brow
But the fish ain't biting tonight.

The hens won't lay and the corn won't grow.
What's wrong with the seasons? Nobody knows.
Somethings up and it won't come down.
What goes around comes around.

I've got to feed a family of four.
Got debt collectors at my door.
Don't know what they're chasing me for
'cause the fish ain't biting tonight.

The hens won't lay and the corn won't grow.
What's wrong with the seasons? Nobody knows.
Somethings up and it won't come down.
What goes around comes around.

Now I wouldn't say that it's ideal,
Trying to make money on a spinning wheel.
I got to find me a better deal
'cause the fish ain't biting tonight.

The hens won't lay and the corn won't grow.

The hens won't lay and the corn won't grow.
What's wrong with the seasons? Nobody knows.
Somethings up and it won't come down.
What goes around comes around.

Snow on the mountain, the sun beats down.
Had all of the seasons rolled into one.
We just have to stick around
And the fish ain't biting tonight.

The hens won't lay and the corn won't grow.
What's wrong with the seasons? Nobody knows.
Somethings up and it won't come down.
What goes around comes around.

It's got about as bad as bad can be.
This old dust bowl is mocking me.
My wife just says "what will be will be".
And the fish ain't biting tonight.

*I read an old southern United States saying which is a term
of acknowledgement of boredom, "Might as well, can't dance, too
wet to plough, fish ain't biting". I was taken by this saying and
began to construct a story behind someone who might have said
this.*

23. Heartbeat of the Moon

Something's come over me, my heart stands still.
She said "never forget me", I never will.
This is an old place, history in its veins.
Sensed the ghosts in its refrains.

I'm not one for going backwards.
That's like flying a lead balloon.
But memories are what made us
The heartbeat of the Moon.

I don't think 'bout those days but I remember them.
It's kind of personal, like a hidden gem.
It's not that I wish that I wasn't here,
But I remember the journey, that made everything so clear.

I'm not one for going backwards.
That's like flying a lead balloon.
But memories are what made us
The heartbeat of the Moon

Tuesdays drag a bit, I don't know why.
There's more going on here than meets the eye.
I visited friends and it helped me to see
That when I look back, I'm just remembering me.

I'm not one for going backwards.
That's like flying a lead balloon.
But memories are what made us
The heartbeat of the Moon

Sometimes I seem to be standing still.
She said "never forget me", I never will.
She said always keep a place in your heart,
Keep my memory in one tiny part.

I'm not one for going backwards.

I'm not one for going backwards.
That's like flying a lead balloon.
But memories are what made us
The heartbeat of the Moon
She said "never forget me"
And I never have.

I wrote this song in late 2018. I had had an overwhelming need to visit my home city of Edinburgh and two of my oldest friends. I don't really know why but I visited some old haunts and spent time with my mates and thoroughly enjoyed myself. This is the song about that experience. So this is my love song to Edinburgh.

24. Transparent

If I could move a mountain and I could sail the seas,
Would it be enough for you to notice me?

I seem to be transparent.
A shadow in the dark.
I've always been and will always be
The ghost you do not see.

If I could turn the tides, fly up to the sun,
Would it be enough for you to know I was the one?

I seem to be transparent.
A shadow in the dark.
I've always been and will always be
The ghost you do not see.

It should be so easy, if we were meant to be.
It would be so obvious for you to notice me.

I seem to be transparent.
A shadow in the dark.
I've always been and will always be
The ghost you do not see.

If I could turn your head, make you hear my voice,
Would it be enough for you to make the right choice?

I seem to be transparent.
A shadow in the dark.
I've always been and will always be
The ghost you do not see.

If I could take dull lead, turn it to golden shine,
Would it be enough to make you mine?

I seem to be transparent.

I seem to be transparent.
A shadow in the dark.
I've always been and will always be
The ghost you do not see.
The ghost you do not see

I've noticed in group situations, such as in the workplace, where one party is smitten by another who is oblivious of the distant yearning. This is someone's story, who has had this experience.

25. How The Pages Fall

I was the one you had a soft spot for.
You left the blame lying at my door.
Left me still wanting more.
I suppose that's just love and war.

Don't want to be your lover, don't want to be your brother.
Let's just see how the pages fall.

I carried anger on my back.
The words written out in coal black.
A code that was too hard to crack.
Bet my money on a shuffled pack.

Don't want to be your lover, don't want to be your brother.
Let's just see how the pages fall.

I said I wanted something to be done.
Everybody looking out for number one.
I suppose it's easier said than done.
I didn't expect you to cut and run.

Don't want to be your lover, don't want to be your brother.
Let's just see how the pages fall.

There is such a power in a group.
One mind jumps through the same hoop.
One thought in an endless loop.
All mixed up in one fell swoop.

Don't want to be your lover, don't want to be your brother.
Let's just see how the pages fall.

I got so angry when he disagreed.

I got so angry when he disagreed.
A friend who thinks the same is a friend indeed.
Truth's just opinion that can mislead.
Much more haste much less speed.

Don't want to be your lover, don't want to be your brother.
Let's just see how the pages fall.
Let's just see how the pages fall.
Let's just see how the pages fall.

*Often, when relationships break down, there is the awkward
explanations phase. Phrases such as "we could still be friends" or
"your just like a brother (or sister) to me" etc are used to soften
the blow. This is a song about that phase of a break up.*

26. Heartbreak Rules

Just in case you thought I didn't think of you
Or thought I'd bitten off more than I could chew.
It's a sad lesson, I'm learning all the rules.
You can't love yourself and love another too.

I'm just travelling in a circle.
I'm just travelling in a circle.
I'm just travelling in a circle.
Heartbreak Rules.
Heartbreak Rules.

Sweet Cinders dancing through the night.
Another fairy tale that always ends up right.
It's sad reality that takes the dream away.
Some fool will say it when there's nothing left to say.

I'm just travelling in a circle.
I'm just travelling in a circle.
I'm just travelling in a circle.
Heartbreak Rules.
Heartbreak Rules.

Words or phrases seem to float around my head.
Then comes an idea with a story instead.
And sometimes stories stay the same, sometimes they just don't.
Life has momentum which is something of its own.

I'm just travelling in a circle.
I'm just travelling in a circle.
I'm just travelling in a circle.
Heartbreak Rules.
Heartbreak Rules.

Just in case you thought I didn't think of you

Just in case you thought I didn't think of you
Or thought I'd bitten off more than I could chew.
It's a sad lesson, I'm learning all the rules.
You can't love yourself and love another too.

I'm just travelling in a circle.
I'm just travelling in a circle.
I'm just travelling in a circle.
Heartbreak Rules.
Heartbreak Rules.
Heartbreak Rules.

I remember reading about the Moscow Rules in a spy novel. They are a set of unwritten guidelines for all spies to follow. It occurred to me that the broken-hearted seem to follow a set of unwritten guidelines which I have called Heartbreak Rules. The words just flowed around the idea and in particular, a phrase I have oft heard, "I seem to be going round and round in circles and getting nowhere".

27. That Old Déjà Vu

I know you turn your phone off late at night
And I can't get to you, try as I might.
You'll be watching catch-ups, sometime on your own.
So, I'll just leave a message for you on your telephone.

Don't get much for a Nickel.
Don't get much for a Dime.
Picked up where I left off.
Just wasting time.

I know you don't want to be disturbed
And all my arguments must sound absurd.
But I just want to be with you, to see it through.
I just got to have some more of that déjà vu.

Don't get much for a Nickel.
Don't get much for a Dime.
Picked up where I left off.
Just wasting time.

I know that you'll be wrapped up warm by now,
On the sofa snuggled down somehow.
But I just want you to know, I've been thinking of you.
So I'll just leave another message déjà vu.

Don't get much for a Nickel.
Don't get much for a Dime.
Picked up where I left off.
Just wasting time.

I know you like to have some time to yourself.
Watching old time movies about romance and wealth.
And I like to have some of that old déjà vu.
So I'll just leave a message so you know I've been thinking of you.
So I'll just leave a message so you know I've been thinking of you.
So I'll just leave a message so you know I've been thinking of you.

I was going to a gig and my wife was staying at home to unwind after a busy couple of days. She was going to put her 'phone on charge and kick back and watch some "catch-ups" on the television. While waiting to go on stage I sent her a message just to say I was thinking of her. I knew she would not see it until the morning but still felt it important. The words to Déjà Vu immediately fell into place and I just finished scribbling them down before going on stage.

28. Solar Sails

It was all so simple; it was all so bright.
As our solar sails harnessed the sun's light.
And the subtle wave of you and me
Drift the heavens like ships through the sea.

Then I turned to her and you looked at him
And we both lost sight of what might have been.
And all that love so serious
Now lies in space between us.

Gossamer sails fly on the sun
Taking us to the stars beyond.
Then a different song we just had to play
And our course began to stray.

When I turned to her and you looked at him
And we both lost sight of what might have been.
And all that love so serious
Now lies in space between us.

The moonbeams floated you away.
Unfinished plans of another day.
The path not taken the choice not made.
You and I were the price we paid.

When I turned to her and you looked at him
And we both lost sight of what might have been.
And all that love so serious
Now lies in space between us.

It was all so simple; it was all so bright.
As our solar sails harnessed the sun's light.
And the subtle wave of you and me
Drift the heavens like ships through the sea.

Then I turned to her and you looked at him

Then I turned to her and you looked at him
And we both lost sight of what might have been.
And all that love so serious
Now lies in space between us.
And all that love so serious
Now lost in space between us.

I was moved by the beauty of CG inspired spacecraft powered by solar sails. I imagined a couple in love sailing the stars. I was thinking of the considerable number of love songs inspired by one of the couple being drawn away to another love. I thought how bitter sweet it would be if both people simultaneously came across someone else and, while wondering which way to go, the existing relationship drifted away without actually ending.

29.   Devil At The Table

The wedding at the Church overlooked the cemetery.
It all seemed rather fitting, I'll tell you why you see.
Neither family liked the other, no one liked the Bride,
Except for the Johnson boy and his best friend Clyde.

Clyde was the best man, he brought along the ring.
A jealous best man's a really dangerous thing.
The service went along well, the boy kissed the girl.
It was about then that things began to unfurl.

At the wedding of the Miller girl to the Johnson boy.
Match made in Hell, just the Devil's joy.
They said that they would pay for it but no one thought that soon.
When the Devil's at your table take a long-handled spoon.

The wedding party went to the local hostelry.
The drink flowed down real easy, some of it was free.
Delores tied on one too many, took some offence,
Said that she was feeling worth about two cents.

At the wedding of the Miller girl to the Johnson boy.
Match made in Hell, just the Devil's joy.
They said that they would pay for it but no one thought that soon.
When the Devil's at your table take a long-handled spoon.

The fight just had to happen, not really any sides.
Fists and feet flying, heads to head collide.
No one at fault, nobody to blame at all.
Once again, back against the wall,

At the wedding of the Miller girl to the Johnson boy.
Match made in Hell, just the Devil's joy.
They said that they would pay for it but no one thought that soon.
When the Devil's at your table take a long-handled spoon.

Delores took out three men then she passed out on the floor.

Delores took out three men then she passed out on the floor.
The Bride and Groom were pushing against an open door.
The Best Man told her that he'd loved her all his life.
And the Johnson boy was suddenly missing one wife.

At the wedding of the Miller girl to the Johnson boy.
Match made in Hell, just the Devil's joy.
They said that they would pay for it but no one thought that soon.
When the Devil's at your table take a long-handled spoon.

There was plenty of damage, like a fight in a saloon.
The boy looked for his wife, could only smell her cheap perfume.
The Miller Girl took off in the Rolls along with Clyde.
The Johnson boy was missing one best friend and a wife.

At the wedding of the Miller girl to the Johnson boy.
Match made in Hell, just the Devil's joy.
They said that they would pay for it but no one thought that soon.
When the Devil's at your table take a long-handled spoon.
When the Devil's at your table take a long-handled spoon.

*My imagined wedding from Hell. I'd love to see a video as I'm
dying to see what Delores looks like!*

30. A Weaver of Time

There's no dreams that hold me,
No wishes on the side.
It's my love that's kept me
Tied up along your side.

If time has mellowed, it has that effect.
I finally turned out to be the man you respect.

Catching those rain tears
Like whispering pearls.
I wouldn't change anything
For all of the world.

If time has mellowed, it has that effect.
I finally turned out to be the man you respect.

Wondering how it walks through.
A weaver of time.
Halfway up this hill,
Together we climb.

If time has mellowed, it has that effect.
I finally turned out to be the man you respect.

There's no chains round my heart
No cage for my soul.
No whispering Judas
With oiled words so droll.

If time has mellowed, it has that effect.
I finally turned out to be the man you respect.

There's no dreams that hold me,
No wishes on the side.
It's my love that's kept me
Tied up along your side.

If time has mellowed, it has that effect.

If time has mellowed, it has that effect.
I finally turned out to be the man you respect.

If you are fortunate, as I have been to be happily married for 20+ years and to be a better person than when you started out because of the love and faith your partner has in you, then you'll understand this song.

31. It'll be alright

Tell me what can I do?
 'Cause I know, 'cause I've been down there too.
And I know that you'll make it through.
There's always me you can turn to.
It'll be alright, it'll be alright.

Come on, can't stay here no more,
 'Cause soon they'll be closing the doors.
You've got to lift up your head,
Never mind the things that they said.
It'll be alright, it'll be alright.

Now I know that you're feeling low.
Things seem all out of control.
Come on and tell me your mind
And tomorrow I think that you'll find
That it's alright, it's going to be alright.

How can I show it to you,
That I have been down there too?
Know that your friends are there
And being there they can share.
If you let them share, it's going to be alright.
It's going to be alright.

This is about having a friend who has given up hope. All you can do is be there.

32. Millennium Waltz

Turn around and you'll find me there like a shadow.
Protecting, moving, wherever you go.
I came with a question seeking an answer.
I found the answer; the answer was you.

Footsteps in the hallway, faces in mirrors
Looking forwards and backwards at once.
Look in the mirror, you'll see me before you,
Behind you, with you wherever you go.
There's a moment when one year is gone not forgotten.
The New Year not ready to quite take its place.
In that moment time stands quite still between us
And you are a heartbeat, a heartbeat away.

Footsteps in the hallway, faces in mirrors
Looking forwards and backwards at once.
Look in the mirror, you'll see me before you,
Behind you, with you wherever you go.

Faces in a mirror frozen in silver
Looking forwards and backwards at once.
In that moment time stands quite still between us
And you are a heartbeat, a heartbeat away.

Footsteps in the hallway, faces in mirrors
Looking forwards and backwards at once.
Look in the mirror, you'll see me before you,
Behind you, with you wherever you go.

There's a moment when one year is gone not forgotten.
The New Year not ready to quite take its place.
In that moment time stands quite still between us
And you are a heartbeat, a heartbeat away.
And you are a heartbeat, a heartbeat away

I wrote this song for New Year 2000. It is a song about the lead up to midnight and takes place in an old-fashioned stately home-type of hotel where the Hogmanay party is being held.

33. The Glamour In You

They said I had it coming, deserved everything I got.
No sympathy for the maverick in me, you choose your own lot.
And I still think the white dress or maybe the blue,
The one with the satin collar, brings out the glamour in you.

I'll tell you tomorrow if I can fly.
I'd really like to make it, so I will try.
Love's no Devil and it's no Saint.
Freedom is bound by its restraint.

Sometimes it takes a stranger, someone you don't know,
To remind you of potential that you once showed.
Somebody laid the road on which you now walk
But that doesn't mean that someone else tells you how to talk.

I'll tell you tomorrow if I can fly.
I'd really like to make it, so I will try.
Love's no Devil and it's no Saint.
Freedom is bound by its restraint.

I can't blame someone else for who I choose to be.
It's my choice to ride the maverick in me.
And one thing above all else is my honesty to myself.
There's got to be rules that you follow when you're a law unto
yourself.

I'll tell you tomorrow if I can fly.
I'd really like to make it, so I will try.
Love's no Devil and it's no Saint.
Freedom is bound by its restraint.

Oh, this place is just the same, as all those years ago.
We may have changed but they stay true, it's a place where I love
to go.
And I still think the white dress or maybe the blue,
The one with the satin collar, brings out the glamour in you.

I'll tell you tomorrow if I can fly.

I'll tell you tomorrow if I can fly.
I'd really like to make it, so I will try.
Love's no Devil and it's no Saint.
Freedom is bound by its restraint.

And the one with the satin collar, brings out the glamour in you.

This is about free spirits and how, later in life, being "tied down"
by love and commitment may not be so bad

34. Edge of the World

Sitting waiting for a train that's gone.
Rain falling all around.
Don't even know where I am
But it feels like the edge of the world.

Even the sleeping hills come awake.
Sunshine leaving shadows in its wake.
Dusty streets, dusty words so to speak.
Well it seems like the edge of the world.

An old man said gallantry's gone.
Not like that when he was a boy.
He said I shouldn't waste my time in this place
'Cause it feels like the edge of the world.

Even the sleeping hills come awake.
Sunshine leaving shadows in its wake.
Dusty streets, dusty words so to speak.
Well it seems like the edge of the world

Who are you to tell me what to do?
Expecting me to listen to you.
Saying if I don't watch I'll end up like you,
Sitting here on the edge of the world.

Even the sleeping hills come awake.
Sunshine leaving shadows in its wake.
Dusty streets, dusty words so to speak.
Well it seems like the edge of the world

You'd think it easy just to turn around.
Just so simple to keep your feet on the ground.
As long as you keep your head in the clouds
You won't stay on the edge of the world.
You won't stay on the edge of the world.
You won't stay on the edge of the world.

I wrote the lyrics to this song about 40 years before I finally came up with the right music, so it shows just how long it can take to write a song! It's based on those films where there is a "one horse town" where the train stops and no one ever gets off. Tumble weed and a stray dog in the street and an old man on a rocking chair.

35. <u>The Letter (to a soldier)</u>

I wanted to write about the horrors of war
But I can't write about somewhere I've never been before.
And I realised what I wanted was the chance to say to you,
Thank you for everything you do.

I know that you signed up for Queen and Country
But the sacrifice you make is for the likes of me.
I just want to say thank you for everything you do.
Just want to tell you I won't forget you.

I'm sure that war's wrong but that's not your call.
You hold our fences strong, back against the wall.
Broken dreams, broken bones, broken hearts,
Broken friends and broken souls.

I know that you signed up for Queen and Country
But the sacrifice you make is for the likes of me.
I just want to say thank you for everything you do.
Just want to tell you I won't forget you.

So, this is the letter that I wrote to you.
I'm not saying I know what you're going through.
You take with you our hearts and minds.
Standing in the space between the lines.

And I know that you signed up for Queen and Country
But the sacrifice you make is for the likes of me.
I just want to say thank you for everything you do.
Just want to tell you I won't forget you.
Just want to tell you we won't forget you.

This song should really be called "a letter to all service personnel, army, navy and air force past and present" but that doesn't really trip off the tongue. So I shortened it!

I regularly watch The Remembrance Day on the TV when not actually attending a ceremony. I am always struck by the fact that the numbers of ex-servicemen from the two World Wars diminishes every year. One year, I can't remember exactly which one, I was watching a parade when the commentator pointed out that there were actually more veterans than before because there had been wars since the Second World War. I am in no way a supporter of war or conflict but am greatly moved by seeing the sacrifice young service people make fighting to preserve the safety of "Queen and Country".

The first specific person I can remember is Simon Weston who, if I remember, is a few years younger than me. He is a veteran of the British Army who suffered severe burn injuries during the Falklands War. I have nothing but admiration for his attitude towards his recovery and the charity work he's done since.

I was also moved to discover that a friend of mine had lost a brother in a recent conflict.

There have been so many souls lost and damaged and I hold them all in such high regard. I decided to write a song about the horror of war but after a year of trying I still had a blank piece of paper. Finally, I realised that I couldn't write a song about war because I have no actual personal experience of it.

I also realised that what I really wanted was simply to tell service people how much I appreciated their sacrifice. So, I sat down and started to write a letter to a service person. I then took my words and sentiments and turned them into this song.

36. **Stand With Angels**

The child was born in a silver flame
And from far and wide the people came.
For hope at last had a name
And we stand with Angels.

I don't believe God's in the sky
And I don't believe Angels fly
But I do believe God's here on Earth
And we stand --- with Angels.

Don't just drift away or trust to fate.
Choose your way before it's too late.
Stand on the shoulders of giants great
And then you can stand with Angels.

I don't believe God's in the sky
And I don't believe Angels fly
But I do believe God's here on Earth
And we stand --- with Angels.

The child was born on the seventh day
And the flame burned down to a silver grey.
For hope will always find a way
Because we --- stand with Angels.

I don't believe God's in the sky
And I don't believe Angels fly
But I do believe God's here on Earth
And that we stand --- with Angels.

He said "I am my Fathers Son.
Goodwill and peace to everyone.
For mankind has only just begun
To stand by the side of Angels

I don't believe God's in the sky

I don't believe God's in the sky
And I don't believe Angels fly
But I do believe God's here on Earth
And we stand with Angels
We can stand with Angels.
Yes we stand with Angels.

I have received care by nurses and doctors and kindness from friends and strangers. I have met people who are kind and helping and have hearts like angels. Gives me a lot of hope.

Part 3
The Chronicles of Jacob Nuntis

I originally wrote "Wind Fall" as a stand-alone song about a wanderer finding himself caught in a small town by a storm. I pictured an old-fashioned tavern, perhaps 18th Century, and this character sitting alone in the corner. He flirts with a barmaid and they have a connection despite the fact that he knows as soon as the wind falls he will be on his way and notwithstanding that he has been warned by a "friendly" regular that she has an "understanding" (an engagement I suppose) with another man.

I became interested in this imaginary character and attempted to write his story with a view to then penning some songs. However, I got lost in a Sci Fi/sword and sorcery story which was not the sort of tale I wanted to tell.

Later, I did some research into Amber. I already knew that Amber was fossilized tree resin and much valued. I read that in the past, in Germany, inhabitants of the shores of an estuary farmed Amber by which I mean they collected it by hand from the shores of a nearby island where Amber was thrown up by the waves in Spring.

This led me to imagine a person owning a large house on an estuary with the rights to farm Amber. He would be rich and held in high regard by local villagers. Such a person would in all probability be courting the most beautiful girl in the village and have everything his material heart desired. Inevitably my story took a turn for the worse and she marries another for love leaving this rich, material man devastated. Abandoning his house and Amber farm he takes to the road (with a haversack of memories and money) to seek happiness.

I wrote a song called "Borderline" and it seemed to me that this was the beginning of the story of the wanderer.

The story was one l fleshed out with "Living Off The Land", where he has become one with nature, "The Chase" where he is nearly caught by those chasing him (probably for some indiscretion with a lady in another town or simply being blamed for something he had not done due to the fear and persecution of outsiders) and "Keeping Moving On" where he says goodbye to the barmaid in "Wind Fall". These three songs were written specifically for this story.

Malcolm Dunn

37. <u>Going To The Borderline</u>

Getting down to the borderline.
Only taking with me what is mine.
A light burning from your chest
Formed by the sun from all that is best.
I remember the days I used to bless.
The colour of my misery's the white of your dress.

I used to live by the estuary,
Farm the leavings of the frozen sea.
You were something I used to possess.
A shining symbol of my success.
But all things change well they do, I guess.
The colour of my misery's the white of your dress.

An amber heart in an embroidered sky.
Cloud faces we personify.
Like the wind and the sun's gold chain.
I open a door; hope I'll see you again.
As faithful as a fool's promise.
The colour of my misery's the white of your dress.

It's ten past seven and I'm moving on.
Nothing to keep me for another morn.
Guess I'll go down to the borderline.
I'll only carry with me what is mine.
A rucksack of memories and sweet distress.
The colour of my misery's the white of your dress.

38. Living Off The Land

I went into town for a drink and company
But by the morning I'll be back up country.
There's a simple truth that they don't understand.
There is such a freedom in living off the land.

People fear what they don't understand.
They think a fist's the same as a helping hand.

I've burned loads of bridges; I'm not going back.
No hesitation, I won't be side-tracked.
There's other motivation than settling down.
There's other destinations than this nothing of a town.

People fear what they don't understand.
They think a fist's the same as a helping hand.

I dread to think of how things might have been.
Living with morals that don't recognise sin.
There's always one who will cast the first stone
On the self-deception of their thorny throne.

People fear what they don't understand.
They think a fist's the same as a helping hand.

I tend to prefer my own company.
It's dreadful waiting to see who'll betray me.
There's some you can trust and there's some will let you down.
Trying to work out which is which in this nothing of a town.

People fear what they don't understand.
They think a fist's the same as a helping hand.

There's a simple truth that they don't understand.
There's such a freedom in living off the land.
There's such a freedom in living off the land.
There's such a freedom in living off the land.

39. <u>Wind Fall</u>

I've money in my pocket I picked up on the road.
There's months enough to keep me if I'm careful with my load.
I cannot stay here for too long or I'll have company
Who'll have questions I don't want to face, backed up with
musketry.

Waiting for a Wind Fall, then I will go on.
I'll not set sail, I'll not depart, in this evil storm.
I cleave to you, I cleave to you, I cleave to you.
But you are promised to another and that will never do.

There's beer and wine a plentiful and cheese with new baked bread
And her smile is waving daintily around my aching head.
But I've heard that she is spoken for, a warning from a friend.
But not the kind that I would ever warmly recommend.

Waiting for a Wind Fall, then I will go on.
I'll not set sail, I'll not depart, in this evil storm.
I cleave to you, I cleave to you, I cleave to you.
But you are promised to another and that will never do.

There's more like me but we don't keep each other's company.
There's danger in such numbers and it's better to be free.
But brothers we are and we lament the passing of our kind
By those who loathe free spirits and prefer the daily grind.

Waiting for a Wind Fall, then I will go on.
I'll not set sail, I'll not depart, in this evil storm.
I cleave to you, I cleave to you, I cleave to you.
But you are promised to another and that will never do.

There's many things I've said and done but few I do regret.
There's none alive left owing to me, I'm in nobody's debt.
But I would take some time with you and I see from your smile
That you would tarry yet with me, a mortal while.

Waiting for a Wind Fall, then I will go on.

Waiting for a Wind Fall, then I will go on.
I'll not set sail, I'll not depart, in this evil storm.
I cleave to you, I cleave to you, I cleave to you.
But you are promised to another and that will never do.

But you would want a wedding ring, a cottage and a hearth
And me to steady down my ways and work the growing earth.
Now that's not my way, though you tempt me to change the life
I've had.
Some are strong and some are weak, some are good and some are
bad.

Waiting for a Wind Fall, then I will go on
I'll not set sail, I'll not depart, in this evil storm.
I cleave to you, I cleave to you, I cleave to you.
But you are promised to another and that will never do.

40. __The Chase__

Just as well I sleep light, I heard a boot on the stair.
Something was wrong, a sound that should not have been there.
Damn, I knew I should have left as soon as the wind fell
And now I'm risking capture and a dank and dusty cell.

Cut to the water, cut to the chase.
I'm headed now to the Devil's hiding place.
In the eye of a storm in the heart of a mouth,
Keep running, keep travelling South.

A drop from the window in the shadows of the lane.
Gather my bag, off and running again.
And the last thing on my mind is her warm and tender smile
As I run like the wind on that moonlit country mile.

Cut to the water, cut to the chase.
I'm headed now to the Devil's hiding place.
In the eye of a storm in the heart of a mouth,
Keep running, keep travelling South.

Those who pursue me get closer to my tail.
But they can't match me, they are going to fail.
There is sanctuary for the likes of me
In the hills and the valleys and the forest of the trees.

Cut to the water, cut to the chase.
I'm headed now to the Devil's hiding place.
In the eye of a storm in the heart of a mouth,
Keep running, keep travelling South.

I have had my fun leading them a merry dance.
They nearly caught me once, now they have had their chance.
I wonder who betrayed me, who let me down?
I know that it was someone in that dirty little town.

Cut to the water, cut to the chase.

Cut to the water, cut to the chase.
I'm headed now to the Devil's hiding place.
In the eye of a storm in the heart of a mouth,
Keep running, keep travelling South.
Keep running, keep travelling South.

41. Keeping Moving On

The storm's abated, there's been Wind Fall.
Time I was moving, if I'm going at all.
I just keep moving on, I just keep moving on.

And I know you'll miss me and I shouldn't sail.
But I've got vigilantes on my tail.
I just keep moving on, just keep moving on.

Now I've been tempted to stay with you.
I cleaved to you but that can never do.
I just keep moving on, I just keep moving on.

I don't look for trouble but it seems to find me.
Like apples that have fallen too far from the tree.
I just keep moving on, just keep moving on.

It's free people like me they can't fence in.
I'm never without but I'm never within.
I just keep moving on, I just keep moving on.

I made no promises to you.
Said when there was Wind Fall I'd be through.
I just keep moving on, just keep moving on.

You were promised to another but that's too bad.
I never wanted to make you sad.
But I'm moving on, just moving on.

It's free people like me they can't fence in.
I'm never without but I'm never within.
I just keep moving on, I just keep moving on.

Don't think I've not been tempted to stay with you.
I cleaved to you but that can never do.
I just keep moving on, just keep moving on.

And I know you'll miss me and I shouldn't sail.

And I know you'll miss me and I shouldn't sail.
But I've got vigilantes on my tail.
I just keep moving on, just keep moving on.

It's free people like me they can't fence in.
I'm never without but I'm never within.
I just keep moving on, I just keep moving on.
I just keep moving on, just keep moving on.
I just keep moving on.